Princess

A Special Polar Bear

A Photo Story by Dennis Fast

Copyright © 2012 by Dennis Fast
First Edition – March 2012

ISBN
978-1-77097-464-7 (Paperback)
978-1-77097-465-4 (eBook)

All rights reserved.

No part of this publication may be reproduced in any form, or by any means, electronic or mechanical, including photocopying, recording, or any information browsing, storage, or retrieval system, without permission in writing from the publisher.

All photographs and text are the property of Dennis Fast and may not be reproduced in any form without written permission from the author except in brief reviews.

Published by:

FriesenPress
Suite 300 – 852 Fort Street
Victoria, BC, Canada V8W 1H8

www.friesenpress.com

Distributed to the trade by The Ingram Book Company

Dedicated to

Frieda, Stuart, Byron and Val

but especially my grandchildren

Ada and Adam

who light up my life.

This is a story just for YOU who may never have seen a wild polar bear.

Maybe YOU have never even been cold.

It is a story told by Uncle Dennis who has been cold many times.

And who has seen many polar bears big and small.

Mostly, though, this is a story about a special polar bear named Princess.

Princess lives in a very cold part of Canada called the Arctic.

In the winter, snow covers the Arctic like sand in the desert.

But for Princess this is home and she really doesn't want to live anywhere else.

Princess loves to watch her caribou neighbours march past in a storm.

And seeing Charlie race by to catch up with his Mom makes her laugh.

Sometimes she laughs till her head aches!

Even her brothers think it is funny.

Alice, the arctic fox, would definitely miss playing with Princess if she would move.

Alice always has a smile for everyone around her.

Susie, the snowy owl, loves adventure so she might follow Princess just to keep her company.

Princess is sure that Patty the ptarmigan would be lonely without her.

Maybe even her wrestling brothers would stop to see her off.

Then, one cold November day, Princess knows she has to go.

Many of her friends are heading out onto the ice of Hudson Bay.

They will be looking for the ringed seal to have their first meal in a long time.

But Princess knows she has to go to a very special place.

She will be going into a soft snow den to have a baby.

It is going to be a long, cold winter under all that snow!

Sometimes Princess dreams of all the smells and food she is missing.

Even a flower would taste good, she thinks.

But sometimes she just dreams of lazy summer afternoons.

Finally, one cold day in March, Princess comes out of her den.

Surprise, she is not alone anymore!

There stands Braveheart with Princess just as proud as can be!

Pretty soon, Wimpy follows them out into their cold new world.

Quickly, Princess leads her cubs to a safe place.

And, before you know it, Braveheart is having a great time.

After a while, Wimpy dares to join Braveheart at play.

But Wimpy is jealous of Braveheart's bigger tree.

So Wimpy tries to take it away, but Braveheart is too strong for him.

Wimpy tries to complain to Mom, but Princess stays calm.

"You should play together," she says to Wimpy, "it's way more fun."

"Ha, ha, Wimpy," Braveheart boasts, "I'm the king of the castle."

I guess it's Braveheart's turn to learn to share.

Princess has heard enough and she calls her cubs to go for a walk.

After a brisk hike, Princess settles down the cubs.

Then she takes a careful look around to make sure they are safe...

...before feeding Braveheart and Wimpy some warm dinner.

By now, Braveheart and Wimpy are getting very tired.

"Good night," Braveheart waves, "we are going to bed."

"Good night, Mom," he says, as he gives her a kiss.

But Wimpy is still grouchy and won't even look at Braveheart.

Pretty soon everyone is snug and warm.

And before you know it, they are fast asleep!

And when the northern lights come out to dance,

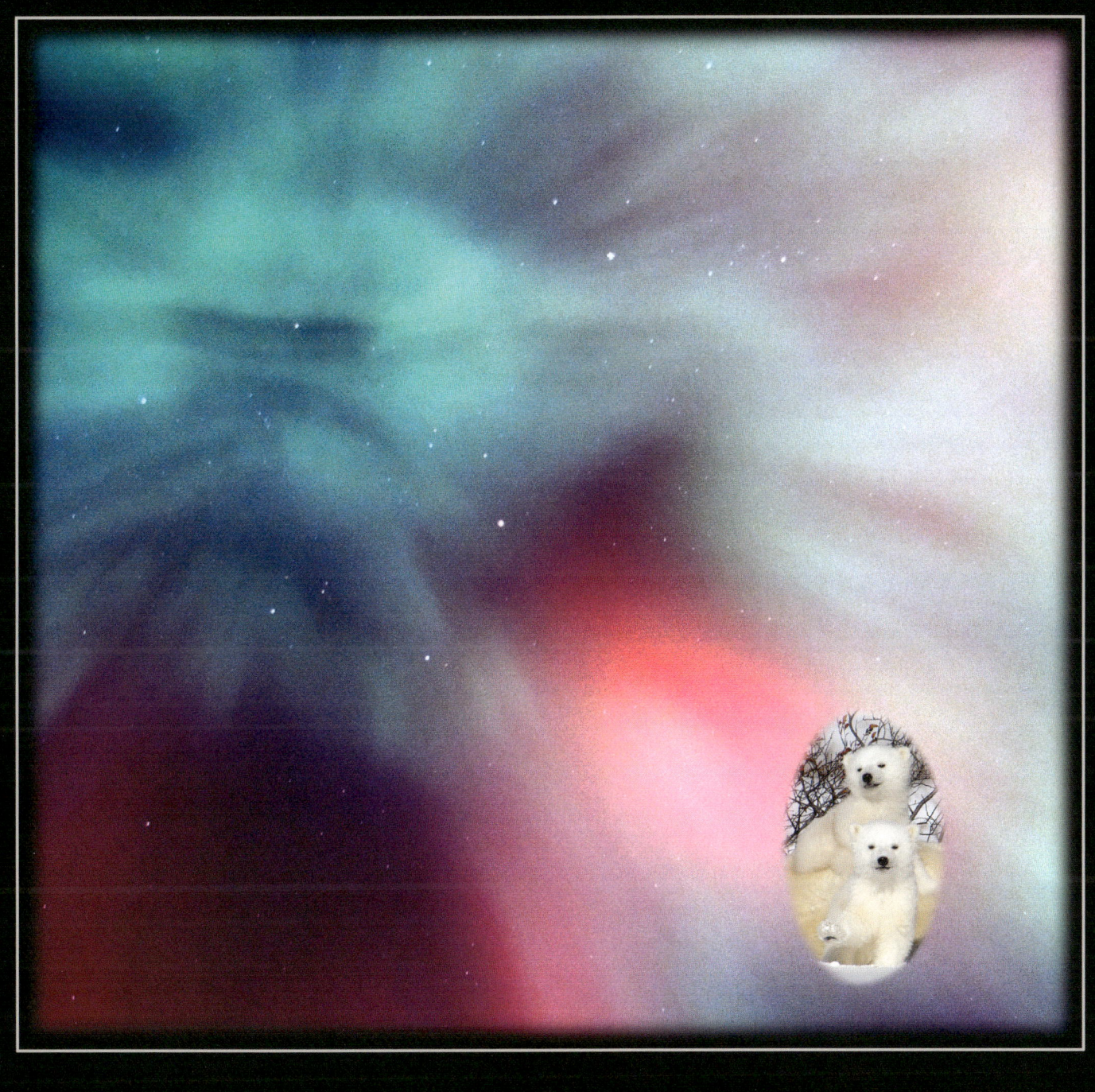

...Braveheart and Wimpy are dreaming of playing just with YOU!

CPSIA information can be obtained
at www.ICGtesting.com
Printed in the USA
LVIW011308130512
281302LV00002B